10-Minute Christmas Crafts for Kids

10-Minute Christmas Crafts for Kids

Matthew Petchinsky

10-minute Christmas Crafts for kids
By: Matthew Petchinsky

Introduction

Welcome and Overview

The holiday season is a magical time of the year when families come together to celebrate, share love, and create lasting memories. One of the most enriching ways to enhance this festive spirit is through crafting—especially when kids are involved. Crafting during Christmas not only adds a personalized touch to your holiday decorations but also creates a warm atmosphere where creativity flourishes, and family bonds are strengthened.

This book, *10-Minute Christmas Crafts for Kids*, is designed to make holiday crafting easy, enjoyable, and accessible for everyone. Each project is simple, requiring minimal materials and time—perfect for busy parents or caregivers looking for fun, engaging activities that children will love. Whether you're decorating your home, creating handmade gifts, or just enjoying a snowy afternoon indoors, these crafts will make your holiday season brighter and more meaningful.

Importance of Holiday Crafts for Kids

Holiday crafts are more than just a fun pastime—they play a crucial role in child development and family connection. For children, crafting is an opportunity to explore their imaginations, develop fine motor skills, and learn how to bring their ideas to life. For parents and caregivers, it's a chance to slow down, engage with their children, and create cherished keepsakes together.

Crafting fosters a sense of accomplishment in kids as they see their creations come to life, whether it's a glittering ornament or a handmade card for a loved one. It also teaches valuable life skills like problem-solving, patience, and the ability to follow instructions—all in a playful and festive context.

Benefits of Crafting: Creativity, Bonding, and Fun

Crafting offers a variety of benefits for both kids and adults:

- **Creativity**: Kids learn to think outside the box, using everyday items like paper plates or toilet paper rolls to make something extraordinary. This imaginative process encourages self-expression and originality.

- **Bonding**: Crafting together provides an opportunity to connect as a family, creating special moments that children will remember long after the holidays are over.
- **Fun**: Holiday crafts are an exciting way to get into the Christmas spirit! The joy of working on a project, seeing it completed, and using it to decorate the house or give as a gift brings smiles to everyone's faces.

Materials Needed for All Crafts (Easy-to-Find Supplies)

To keep things simple and stress-free, the crafts in this book rely on materials you likely already have at home or can easily find at your local store. Here's a quick list of the essentials:

- **Basic Supplies**: Construction paper, markers, crayons, glue, tape, scissors (safety scissors for younger kids), and a ruler
- **Craft Items**: Glitter, pom-poms, googly eyes, pipe cleaners, popsicle sticks, and beads
- **Recycled Materials**: Toilet paper rolls, paper plates, coffee filters, old socks, and mason jar lids
- **Seasonal Touches**: Red and green ribbons, metallic paint, cupcake liners, and holiday-themed stickers

By having these items on hand, you'll be prepared for every craft in this book, without needing to make extra trips to the store.

How to Keep Crafts Quick and Mess-Free

One of the most common concerns about crafting with kids is the potential for mess. With a little preparation and a few smart strategies, you can minimize the cleanup and keep the focus on fun:

1. **Create a Craft Station**: Set up a designated crafting area with easy-to-clean surfaces, like a kitchen table or a plastic tablecloth.
2. **Organize Materials**: Use bins or trays to keep supplies sorted and within reach, so kids don't have to rummage around.
3. **Use Recyclable or Disposable Items**: Paper plates, coffee filters, and cupcake liners make great bases for crafts and can be easily tossed after use.
4. **Supervise Without Overmanaging**: Guide younger kids to use supplies safely and responsibly while letting them take ownership of their projects.
5. **Quick Cleanup Tips**: Keep a small trash bag and wet wipes nearby to manage spills and scraps as they happen.

Tips for Encouraging Kids' Independence in Crafting

Crafting is an excellent way for children to practice independence and develop confidence in their abilities. Here's how you can foster this sense of autonomy:

- **Offer Choices**: Let kids pick the craft they want to do and encourage them to make decisions about colors, materials, and designs.
- **Provide Simple Instructions**: Give step-by-step guidance that's easy for kids to follow, but leave room for their creativity to shine.
- **Celebrate Their Efforts**: Praise kids for their hard work and creativity, focusing on the joy of the process rather than perfection.
- **Teach Basic Skills**: Show kids how to safely use scissors, apply glue, or measure materials, empowering them to take on more complex tasks.

- **Encourage Teamwork**: If working with siblings or friends, teach kids to collaborate and share materials, fostering cooperation and patience.

This introduction sets the stage for a crafting adventure that's as rewarding as it is festive. Each chapter will guide you through quick and delightful projects, ensuring that you and your children make the most of your holiday season. Let's get started!

Chapter 1: Paper Plate Snowmen

Snowmen are one of the most iconic symbols of winter and Christmas. This craft allows kids to bring the magic of snowmen indoors, using simple materials like paper plates and a touch of creativity. In just 10 minutes, your child can create a cheerful paper plate snowman to decorate the house or gift to someone special.

Materials Needed

For one snowman, you'll need:

- **2 white paper plates** (one large for the body, one small for the head)
- **Black construction paper** (for the hat and buttons)
- **Orange construction paper** (for the carrot nose)
- **Markers or crayons** (black for eyes and mouth, any color for decorative touches)
- **Glue or tape**
- **Scissors**
- **Cotton balls or pom-poms** (optional for added texture)
- **Scraps of fabric or ribbon** (for the scarf)
- **Twigs or pipe cleaners** (for arms, optional)

Step-by-Step Guide to Turning Paper Plates into Cheerful Snowmen

1. **Prepare the Base**
   - Take one large paper plate (the body) and one small paper plate (the head).
   - Place the smaller plate slightly overlapping the top edge of the larger plate, resembling a snowman. Use glue or tape to attach them together.
2. **Create the Face**
   - On the smaller plate, use a black marker or crayon to draw two round eyes.
   - Cut a triangle out of orange construction paper for the carrot nose and glue it in the center of the face.
   - Draw a smile with small dots or a curved line beneath the nose.
3. **Add Buttons**
   - Cut small circles out of black construction paper or use pom-poms to make buttons for the snowman's body.
   - Glue or tape 2–3 buttons down the center of the larger paper plate.
4. **Make the Hat**
   - Cut a rectangle and a thin strip from black construction paper to form the snowman's hat.
   - Attach the hat to the top of the smaller plate with glue or tape.
   - For a festive touch, decorate the hat with a strip of red ribbon or draw designs with markers.

5. **Dress with a Scarf**
   - Cut a strip of fabric or ribbon to use as the snowman's scarf.
   - Wrap the scarf around the "neck" where the two plates meet. Secure it with glue or tie it loosely in place.
6. **Optional: Add Arms**
   - Use small twigs or pipe cleaners to create the snowman's arms.
   - Attach one twig or pipe cleaner to each side of the larger plate with tape or glue.
7. **Decorate and Customize**
   - Let your child add any additional decorations they like. They can use cotton balls for snow, glitter for sparkle, or stickers for extra flair.

Variations for Adding Hats, Scarves, and Arms

1. **Hats**
   - **Top Hat**: Use black construction paper to make a classic top hat. Add a holly leaf and berries cut from green and red paper for a festive touch.
   - **Santa Hat**: Make a triangular Santa hat from red construction paper and add a white pom-pom and a cotton ball trim.
   - **Beanie Hat**: Cut a curved shape out of colored construction paper and add a fuzzy pom-pom on top.

2. **Scarves**
   - **Fabric Scraps**: Use bright holiday-patterned fabric for an extra Christmassy look.
   - **Yarn Tassels**: Tie together strands of yarn to create a tassel effect on the ends of the scarf.
   - **Paper Scarf**: Draw and cut out a scarf from construction paper and let the kids color in patterns like stripes or polka dots.

3. **Arms**
   - **Natural Twigs**: Gather small twigs from outside and glue or tape them to the sides of the snowman for a rustic look.
   - **Pipe Cleaners**: Bend brown or black pipe cleaners into arm shapes, adding small loops at the ends to mimic hands.
   - **Construction Paper Arms**: Cut out simple arm shapes from black or brown paper and glue them onto the snowman.

Tips for Success

- **Encourage Creativity**: Let kids make their snowmen unique by choosing their own colors and decorations.
- **Prepare Materials Ahead**: Pre-cutting small pieces like buttons or scarf strips can make the process quicker for younger children.
- **Layer Glue Sparingly**: Remind kids to use a small amount of glue to avoid a mess and allow their creations to dry quickly.

With this simple craft, your child will create a festive snowman full of personality! Display their work on the refrigerator, hang it on a wall, or use it as part of a Christmas centerpiece. These paper plate snowmen are sure to bring holiday cheer to your home.

Chapter 2: Popsicle Stick Christmas Trees

Popsicle stick Christmas trees are a simple, creative, and budget-friendly craft that kids can make in just a few minutes. These tiny, colorful trees can be turned into ornaments, gift tags, or stand-alone decorations. With endless customization options, each tree will be a unique masterpiece that reflects your child's creativity.

Materials Needed

For one popsicle stick Christmas tree, you'll need:

- **3 popsicle sticks** (or colored craft sticks)
- **Green paint or markers** (optional for coloring the sticks)
- **Glue (hot glue for older kids or craft glue for younger ones)**
- **Mini pom-poms, beads, or buttons** (for ornaments)
- **Glitter or glitter glue**
- **Sequins or rhinestones**
- **Brown construction paper or a small piece of a popsicle stick** (for the tree trunk)
- **Star stickers, foam stars, or cut-out paper stars** (for the tree topper)
- **String or ribbon** (if you want to hang it as an ornament)

How to Make Colorful and Customizable Trees Using Popsicle Sticks

1. **Create the Tree Shape**
   - Take three popsicle sticks and arrange them into a triangle to form the outline of the Christmas tree.
   - Glue the ends of the sticks together where they meet. Allow the glue to dry for a few minutes.
   - For younger kids, pre-glue the triangles to make assembly quicker and easier.
2. **Paint or Color the Sticks**
   - Use green paint, markers, or crayons to color the popsicle sticks.
   - For an extra festive touch, let kids add a layer of glitter glue over the green paint or sprinkle loose glitter onto wet glue for a sparkling effect.
3. **Add the Tree Trunk**
   - Cut a small rectangle from brown construction paper or use a small piece of a popsicle stick for the tree trunk.
   - Attach it to the bottom of the triangle with glue.
4. **Decorate the Tree**
   - Let your child's imagination shine as they decorate their tree:
     - **Mini Ornaments**: Glue on pom-poms, beads, or buttons to mimic ornaments.
     - **Garlands**: Use strands of yarn, string, or thin ribbon as garlands, draping them across the tree.
     - **Rhinestones and Sequins**: Add sparkle with sequins or rhinestones to make the tree shimmer.
     - **Snow Effect**: Dab small bits of white paint or glue on the sticks and sprinkle glitter for a snow-dusted look.

5. **Top It Off with a Star**
   - Add a star sticker, foam star, or a small star cut from yellow construction paper to the top of the tree. Glue it securely in place.
6. **Optional: Turn It Into an Ornament**
   - To make the tree hangable, glue a loop of ribbon or string to the back of the tree. Allow it to dry completely before hanging on the Christmas tree.

Decorating Ideas with Pom-Poms, Glitter, and Mini Ornaments

1. **Classic Christmas Look**
   - Use traditional red and green mini pom-poms for ornaments and a gold or silver star on top. Add fine glitter to the tree's edges for a frosted appearance.

2. **Whimsical Rainbow Tree**
   - Paint the popsicle sticks in different bright colors. Decorate with multicolored rhinestones and sequins for a playful, rainbow-inspired tree.

3. **Rustic Charm**
   - Leave the popsicle sticks unpainted for a natural wood look. Use twine for garlands and tiny wooden beads as ornaments. Add a burlap star on top for a rustic vibe.

4. **Winter Wonderland Tree**
   - Paint the sticks white or light blue to mimic a snowy tree. Decorate with silver glitter, white pom-poms, and snowflake stickers for a frosty theme.

5. **Personalized Keepsake Tree**
   - Add a personal touch by including the child's name or the year on the tree. Use metallic markers to write directly on the popsicle sticks or on a small ornament glued to the tree.

6. **Miniature Ornament Tree**
   - Attach mini jingle bells, tiny bows, or small holiday charms as ornaments for a more detailed look.

Tips for Crafting Success

- **Organize the Materials**: Place all decorating supplies in small bowls or containers so kids can easily choose their items.
- **Use Age-Appropriate Glue**: Hot glue is faster and more durable but should only be used by older kids or adults. Younger kids can use craft glue with some assistance.
- **Encourage Experimentation**: Remind kids there's no right or wrong way to decorate their tree. Each tree is unique, just like snowflakes!
- **Quick Drying Tips**: If you're short on time, use a fan or hairdryer on a low setting to speed up the drying process.

Popsicle stick Christmas trees are versatile, fun, and easy to make, making them a perfect project for kids of all ages. Whether they're used as ornaments, gift tags, or displayed on a shelf, these tiny trees are sure to bring festive cheer to your home. Let the creativity begin!

Chapter 3: Handprint Reindeer

Handprint crafts are a timeless favorite because they capture a child's unique size and shape, creating a keepsake that families can cherish forever. Handprint reindeer art is a simple, heartwarming project that transforms your child's handprints into adorable reindeer with festive red noses. This craft is quick, fun, and perfect for holiday cards, decorations, or gifts.

Materials Needed

For one handprint reindeer craft, you'll need:

- **Brown construction paper** (or white paper with brown paint/ markers)
- **Black marker or crayon**
- **Red pom-poms or red construction paper** (for the nose)
- **Googly eyes**
- **Glue or tape**
- **Scissors**
- **Additional decorations** (optional: glitter, stickers, small bows, etc.)
- **Optional: White cardstock** (for framing the reindeer or making a card)

Using Kids' Handprints to Create Adorable Reindeer Art

1. **Prepare the Materials**
   - Lay out the construction paper, glue, markers, and other supplies.
   - If you're using white paper, have brown paint or markers ready for coloring.
2. **Trace the Handprints**
   - Have your child place one hand on the brown construction paper.
   - Using a black marker or pencil, trace around their hand. Repeat for the other hand.
   - If your child prefers, they can press their hand into brown paint and stamp it directly onto the paper.
3. **Cut Out the Handprints**
   - Carefully cut out the handprint shapes. These will form the reindeer's antlers.
4. **Create the Reindeer's Head**
   - Cut an oval or teardrop shape out of brown construction paper for the reindeer's head. Make it slightly larger than the handprints.
5. **Assemble the Reindeer**
   - Glue the two handprints to the top corners of the reindeer's head, with fingers pointing outward. These are the antlers.
   - Attach the reindeer's head to a piece of white cardstock if you're making a card or frame.
6. **Add the Face**
   - Glue googly eyes near the center of the reindeer's head.
   - Attach a red pom-pom or circle of red construction paper to the bottom center for the nose.
   - Use a black marker to draw a friendly smile or add extra details like freckles or eyelashes.

Adding Googly Eyes and Red Noses for a Festive Touch

1. **Googly Eyes**
   - Choose medium-sized googly eyes that are easy to handle for little hands.
   - For a fun twist, use googly eyes with eyelashes or colorful borders.
   - If you don't have googly eyes, draw large eyes with a black marker and add a white highlight for a cute, cartoonish look.

2. **Red Nose Options**
   - **Pom-Poms**: Use a fluffy red pom-pom for Rudolph's signature nose. These add texture and dimension to the craft.
   - **Paper Cut-Out**: If you don't have pom-poms, cut a small circle out of red construction paper.
   - **Glitter Nose**: Draw a circle with glue where the nose will go, sprinkle red glitter on top, and let it dry.

3. **Festive Extras**
   - Add a small bow under the reindeer's face for a festive touch. Use ribbon, pre-made mini bows, or cut one from red paper.
   - Use glitter glue to outline the antlers or create sparkling snowflakes around the reindeer.

Creative Variations for Handprint Reindeer Art

1. **Reindeer Family**
   - Create a whole family of reindeer by tracing each family member's handprints. Use the largest handprint for the parent reindeer and smaller ones for the kids.
2. **Personalized Reindeer Cards**
   - Turn the handprint reindeer into a holiday card by gluing it onto folded cardstock. Inside, write a heartfelt message and let your child decorate with stickers or stamps.
3. **Ornaments**
   - Shrink the design by tracing smaller handprints and use lightweight cardstock. Attach a loop of ribbon to the back to turn it into a tree ornament.
4. **Framed Keepsake**
   - Mount the handprint reindeer on a festive background, such as holiday-themed scrapbook paper. Add the child's name and date, and frame it as a holiday keepsake.

Tips for Success

1. **Choose the Right Paper**
   - Use sturdy construction paper or cardstock to ensure the reindeer holds its shape, especially if it will be framed or hung as a decoration.
2. **Encourage Creativity**
   - Allow kids to personalize their reindeer by adding unique features, such as patterned antlers, silly faces, or sparkly details.
3. **Manage Messes**
   - If using paint, place a plastic tablecloth or old newspaper under your work area to catch spills. Have wet wipes or a damp cloth nearby for quick cleanup.

4. **Make It Interactive**
   - While assembling the reindeer, talk with your child about the story of Rudolph and his red nose or play holiday music to make the activity even more festive.

Handprint reindeer crafts are a wonderful way to combine creativity with the holiday spirit. Not only are they fun to make, but they also capture a moment in time, preserving your child's tiny handprint for years to come. Whether displayed on the fridge, framed on the wall, or sent as a heartfelt holiday card, these reindeer are sure to bring smiles and festive cheer to everyone who sees them!

Chapter 4: Toilet Paper Roll Santas

Toilet paper roll Santas are a delightful way to upcycle everyday household items into charming Christmas decorations. This craft is eco-friendly, simple, and provides endless opportunities for kids to get creative. By transforming an ordinary toilet paper roll into a jolly Santa, children can learn about reusing materials while making adorable holiday decor.

Materials Needed

For one Santa, you'll need:

- **Empty toilet paper roll**
- **Red construction paper or red paint**
- **White construction paper or cotton balls** (for the beard and trim)
- **Black construction paper** (for the belt)
- **Yellow construction paper or marker** (for the belt buckle)
- **Googly eyes**
- **Small pink or peach circle of paper** (for the face)
- **Glue stick, craft glue, or hot glue (with supervision)**
- **Scissors**
- **Optional**: Glitter, stickers, or a small pom-pom for the hat

Crafting Santas with Upcycled Materials

1. **Prepare the Toilet Paper Roll**
   - Clean and smooth the edges of the toilet paper roll to ensure it's ready for crafting.
   - Optionally, you can paint the roll red for a vibrant base or cover it with red construction paper for a smoother finish.

2. **Wrap the Roll in Santa's Coat**
   - Cut a strip of red construction paper long enough to wrap around the roll.
   - Glue or tape the paper to the roll, ensuring it's snug and evenly aligned. If using paint, let it dry completely before moving to the next step.

3. **Add Santa's Face**
   - Cut a small oval or circle from pink or peach-colored paper for Santa's face.
   - Glue the face onto the roll, positioning it about one-third of the way down from the top edge.

4. **Make Santa's Beard**
   - Cut a beard shape from white construction paper or use cotton balls for a fluffy texture.
   - Glue the beard below Santa's face, letting it cover the lower half of the oval.
   - For extra fun, add a curly mustache made of small white paper strips or cotton.

5. **Attach Googly Eyes**
   - Glue two googly eyes onto the face, slightly above the beard.
   - If you don't have googly eyes, draw eyes with a black marker or use small black circles cut from construction paper.

6. **Add Santa's Hat**
    - Cut a triangle from red construction paper to form the hat.
    - Roll the triangle into a cone shape and glue the edges together.
    - Attach the hat to the top of the roll, slightly tilted for a whimsical look. Add a small white pom-pom or cotton ball to the tip of the hat.

7. **Create Santa's Trim**
    - Cut a strip of white construction paper or use cotton balls to make the trim for Santa's coat.
    - Glue the trim around the bottom and top edges of the roll.

8. **Add the Belt and Buckle**
    - Cut a thin strip of black construction paper for the belt. Wrap it around the middle of the roll and glue it in place.
    - Cut a small square from yellow construction paper, then cut out the center to create a buckle shape. Attach it to the front of the belt.

Painting, Cutting, and Gluing Tips for Little Hands

1. **Painting Tips**
   - Use washable red paint for easy cleanup.
   - Provide a wide paintbrush with soft bristles, which is easier for small hands to control.
   - Let the roll sit on a piece of wax paper while drying to prevent sticking or smudging.

2. **Cutting Tips**
   - Use safety scissors designed for children.
   - Pre-cut small or intricate shapes (like the buckle or beard) for younger children to make the process faster and safer.
   - Encourage older children to trace shapes on construction paper before cutting, helping them develop fine motor skills.

3. **Gluing Tips**
   - Use a glue stick for paper pieces, as it's less messy and easier to handle.
   - For cotton balls or heavier decorations, craft glue is more effective. Supervise if using hot glue for sturdier attachment.
   - Show children how to apply small amounts of glue to prevent messes and speed up drying time.

Creative Variations

1. **Sparkling Santa**
   - Add glitter to Santa's coat or hat for a sparkling effect. Apply glue in small areas and sprinkle glitter over it, then shake off the excess.
2. **Santa Family**
   - Create Santas in different sizes by using cardboard tubes from paper towels or wrapping paper. These can represent a whole family of Santas.
3. **Interactive Santa**
   - Glue a small magnet to the back of the roll to turn it into a fridge decoration.
   - Attach a ribbon to the top to make it a hanging ornament.
4. **Gift Holder Santa**
   - Turn the Santa into a small gift container by placing candy or trinkets inside the roll and sealing one end with paper or fabric.

Tips for Success

1. **Set Up a Craft Station**
   - Lay down a tablecloth or old newspaper to catch glue and paint spills.
   - Arrange materials in small containers or bowls for easy access.
2. **Encourage Personalization**
   - Let kids customize their Santas with stickers, buttons, or colored markers.
   - Suggest fun details like rosy cheeks (with pink crayon) or glittery snowflakes on Santa's coat.
3. **Make It a Group Activity**

- If crafting with siblings or friends, encourage each child to create a unique Santa to share with the group.

Toilet paper roll Santas are a fantastic way to introduce kids to the joy of upcycling while fostering their creativity and dexterity. These cheerful Santas can be used as decorations, ornaments, or thoughtful gifts, bringing festive fun to your home while teaching valuable lessons about resourcefulness and imagination.

Chapter 5: Pipe Cleaner Candy Canes

Pipe cleaner candy canes are a classic and fun craft that's perfect for kids of all ages. They're easy to make, require minimal materials, and are incredibly versatile. Whether used as tree ornaments, gift toppers, or decorations, these candy canes add a festive touch to the holidays while helping children develop their creativity and fine motor skills.

Materials Needed

For each candy cane, you'll need:

- **Pipe cleaners in red and white** (or other festive colors)
- **Optional: Green, gold, silver, or glittery pipe cleaners**
- **Scissors** (optional for cutting pipe cleaners to size)
- **String or ribbon** (if making hanging ornaments)

Twisting Pipe Cleaners into Candy Cane Shapes

1. **Choose Your Pipe Cleaners**
   - Start with one red pipe cleaner and one white pipe cleaner for a traditional candy cane look.
   - For a twist on tradition, use other color combinations like green and silver, red and gold, or even rainbow colors.
2. **Align the Pipe Cleaners**
   - Hold the two pipe cleaners together so their ends are aligned.
3. **Twist the Pipe Cleaners Together**
   - Begin twisting the pipe cleaners around each other, starting at one end.
   - Continue twisting down the length of the pipe cleaners, keeping the twists tight and even to create a neat striped pattern.

- Adjust as needed to ensure the colors are evenly distributed.

4. Shape into a Candy Cane

- Once fully twisted, gently bend the twisted pipe cleaner into a candy cane shape, forming a hook at one end.

5. Trim if Necessary

- If the candy cane is too long, use scissors to trim the bottom to your desired length.

Combining Colors for a Unique Design

1. Traditional Red and White

- Stick with classic red and white for a timeless candy cane design.

2. Festive Green and Red

- Use green and red pipe cleaners for a variation that still feels Christmassy.

3. Sparkly Candy Canes

- Incorporate glittery or metallic pipe cleaners to add shimmer and shine. For example, pair a red pipe cleaner with a gold or silver glitter pipe cleaner.

4. Rainbow Candy Canes

- For a colorful and whimsical twist, use multiple colors like blue, pink, yellow, and green.

5. Winter Wonderland Theme

- Use white and light blue pipe cleaners for a frosty, snow-inspired design. Add a glittery silver pipe cleaner for extra sparkle.

6. Personalized Colors

- Let kids choose their favorite color combinations to make candy canes that reflect their unique personalities.

Creative Uses for Pipe Cleaner Candy Canes

1. Tree Ornaments
- Attach a small loop of string or ribbon to the top of the candy cane, then hang it on the Christmas tree.

2. Gift Toppers
- Tuck a candy cane into the bow on a wrapped gift for a festive, handmade touch.

3. Garlands
- Make multiple candy canes and string them together to create a decorative garland for your home or classroom.

4. Place Card Holders
- Use candy canes to hold place cards at holiday dinners. Bend the hook slightly to grip the card securely.

5. Party Favors
- Hand out the candy canes as party favors during holiday gatherings or classroom celebrations.

Tips for Crafting Success

1. Ensure Even Twists
- Demonstrate how to twist the pipe cleaners evenly so the stripes look neat. Younger kids may need guidance with this step.

2. Secure the Ends
- Tuck the ends of the pipe cleaners inward to avoid sharp edges that might poke little fingers.

3. Encourage Creativity
- Let kids experiment with colors and shapes. Some might enjoy making spiral or heart-shaped candy canes.

4. Make It a Group Activity

- This craft is quick and simple, making it ideal for group settings like classrooms, playdates, or family gatherings.

5. **Use High-Quality Pipe Cleaners**
   - Choose sturdy, flexible pipe cleaners that hold their shape well. Thin or flimsy ones may not twist as effectively.

Variations for Advanced Crafters

1. **Beaded Candy Canes**
   - Thread small, colorful beads onto the pipe cleaners before twisting them together. The beads add texture and an extra layer of detail.
2. **Mini Candy Canes**
   - Cut the pipe cleaners into smaller lengths and follow the same steps to create mini versions. These are perfect for decorating dollhouses or as tiny ornaments.
3. **Candy Cane Shapes with a Twist**
   - Twist two or more candy canes together to form larger shapes like a wreath or a heart.
4. **Candy Cane Characters**
   - Add googly eyes and small felt pieces to turn the candy canes into whimsical characters like elves or reindeer.

Pipe cleaner candy canes are the perfect blend of simplicity and creativity, making them an ideal holiday craft for kids. They're easy to customize, fun to create, and can be used in countless ways to enhance your holiday decorations. Let your kids' imaginations run wild as they twist, shape, and design their own candy cane creations!

Chapter 6: Paper Chain Garland

Paper chain garlands are a timeless holiday craft that's easy to create, fun to customize, and perfect for decorating your home. This simple project uses strips of paper to make interlocking loops that can be hung on Christmas trees, across mantels, or anywhere else that could use a festive touch. It's a great craft for kids of all ages and encourages creativity through color and pattern choices.

Materials Needed

For a paper chain garland, you'll need:

- **Construction paper or colored paper** (red, green, white, or any festive colors)
- **Scissors or paper cutter**
- **Glue stick, tape, or stapler**
- **Optional: Markers, stickers, or glitter** (for decorating the strips)

Simple Instructions for Making Decorative Paper Chains

1. **Prepare the Paper Strips**
   - Cut construction paper into strips that are approximately **1 inch wide and 6 inches long**. This size works well for making loops that are easy to handle and visually appealing.
   - For younger children, pre-cut the strips to make the process quicker and easier.
2. **Make the First Loop**
   - Take one strip of paper and form it into a circle, overlapping the ends slightly.
   - Secure the ends using glue, tape, or a stapler. (Glue sticks are ideal for mess-free crafting, while tape and staples provide instant results.)

3. **Add the Next Link**
   - Take another strip of paper, slide it through the first loop, and form it into a circle.
   - Secure the ends of the second strip as you did with the first.
4. **Continue the Chain**
   - Repeat the process, linking one strip through the previous loop and securing it until the chain reaches your desired length.
5. **Finish and Display**
   - Once your chain is complete, decide where you'd like to hang or drape it. Paper chain garlands look great on Christmas trees, along stair railings, or framing doorways and windows.

Fun Patterns and Festive Color Combinations

1. **Traditional Christmas Colors**
   - Use red and green paper for a classic holiday look. Alternate the colors for a striped effect, or add white paper for a "candy cane" pattern.
2. **Winter Wonderland Theme**
   - Use white, light blue, and silver paper to create a frosty, snow-inspired garland. Add glitter or metallic accents for extra sparkle.
3. **Bright and Cheerful**
   - Incorporate bold colors like pink, purple, or turquoise to create a whimsical, non-traditional holiday theme.
4. **Patterned Paper**
   - Use patterned scrapbook paper featuring holiday designs like snowflakes, Christmas trees, or reindeer for a more intricate and festive appearance.
5. **Personalized Chain**

◦ Decorate the strips before assembling the chain. Kids can draw pictures, write holiday wishes, or add stickers to make the garland uniquely theirs.

6. **Countdown Garland**
   ◦ Turn the paper chain into an advent calendar by labeling each loop with a number (e.g., 1–25). Remove one link each day as you count down to Christmas.

7. **Mixed Materials**
   ◦ Combine construction paper with strips of ribbon, fabric, or metallic foil to add texture and variety to your garland.

Creative Uses for Paper Chain Garland

1. **Christmas Tree Decor**
   ◦ Wrap the paper chain around the tree as a festive alternative to traditional tinsel or lights.

2. **Room Decorations**
   ◦ Hang the garland along walls, windows, or door frames to instantly brighten any space.

3. **Table Centerpiece**
   ◦ Drape the chain across the center of your dining table for a playful and colorful table runner.

4. **Gift Wrapping**
   ◦ Use shorter chains to wrap around presents or create unique gift toppers.

5. **Classroom Projects**
   ◦ Collaborate with classmates to create a giant paper chain garland for a school event or holiday party.

6. **Themed Party Decor**
   ◦ Tailor the colors and patterns to match the theme of a holiday party, such as a gingerbread or candy land theme.

Tips for Crafting Success

1. **Use Sturdy Paper**
   - Choose construction paper or cardstock for durability, especially if the garland will be handled frequently or hung outdoors.
2. **Pre-Cut Strips for Younger Kids**
   - For smaller children, prepare the paper strips in advance to streamline the process and avoid frustration.
3. **Experiment with Sizes**
   - Try making chains with different strip lengths and widths for unique looks. Thicker loops are bold and eye-catching, while thinner loops create a delicate effect.
4. **Plan Your Pattern**
   - Lay out the paper strips in the desired order before assembling the chain to ensure a consistent pattern.
5. **Make It a Group Activity**
   - Paper chains are perfect for group settings. Assign each person a task (cutting, linking, securing) to make the craft collaborative and fun.

Advanced Variations

1. **Double Chains**
   - Create two paper chains and twist them together for a braided effect.
2. **Mini Garland**
   - Make a tiny version of the chain using smaller strips of paper to decorate miniature Christmas trees or dollhouses.
3. **Starry Links**
   - Cut star shapes into the paper strips before linking them to add a celestial twist to your garland.

4. **Light-Up Chain**
   - Weave a string of LED fairy lights through the chain to create a glowing garland for evening displays.

Paper chain garlands are a fantastic way to combine creativity, teamwork, and festive fun. Their simplicity makes them an excellent choice for young crafters, while the endless design possibilities keep the craft exciting for older children and adults. Whether you stick with traditional red and green or explore unique patterns and colors, your paper chain garland is sure to add warmth and cheer to your holiday celebrations.

Chapter 7: Cupcake Liner Angels

Cupcake liner angels are a charming and easy-to-make craft that brings a touch of grace to holiday decorations. These delicate angels are perfect for Christmas trees, table centerpieces, or as heartfelt handmade gifts. Using cupcake liners, beads, and a few simple materials, children can create beautiful angels and customize them to their liking.

Materials Needed

For one cupcake liner angel, you'll need:

- **2–3 cupcake liners** (white, gold, silver, or patterned)
- **1 medium-sized wooden bead** (for the head)
- **1 pipe cleaner** (for the halo)
- **Glue or hot glue** (for secure assembly)
- **String or ribbon** (if making a hanging ornament)
- **Markers or paint** (to decorate the bead or liners, optional)
- **Glitter, rhinestones, or sequins** (for embellishments)
- **Optional: Small feather pieces or lace** (for extra wing details)

Creating Angels with Cupcake Liners and Beads

1. **Prepare the Cupcake Liners**
   - Flatten one cupcake liner to create the angel's skirt.
   - If desired, fold the skirt liner slightly to create pleats for a textured appearance.
   - Set another liner aside to use for the angel's wings.
2. **Create the Body**
   - Roll a third cupcake liner into a small cone shape for the angel's body.

○ Glue or tape the cone to hold its shape, then glue it onto the center of the skirt liner.

3. **Add the Head**

   ○ Attach the wooden bead to the top of the cone to form the angel's head. Use glue to secure it firmly.

   ○ If desired, use a marker or paint to draw a face on the bead. Add eyes, a small smile, or rosy cheeks.

4. **Attach the Wings**

   ○ Take the second cupcake liner and fold it in half. Then, fold it again into a triangular shape to create the wings.

   ○ Glue the folded liner to the back of the angel's body. Adjust the wings to fan out slightly for a graceful look.

5. **Create the Halo**

   ○ Bend the pipe cleaner into a small circle to form the halo.

   ○ Attach the halo to the back of the bead using glue or by wrapping the remaining pipe cleaner around the top of the cone.

6. **Add a Loop for Hanging (Optional)**

   ○ If making an ornament, glue or tie a piece of string or ribbon to the back of the angel's head or body.

7. **Decorate the Angel**

   ○ Use glitter glue, rhinestones, or sequins to embellish the skirt and wings. Add a touch of sparkle to make the angel stand out.

Customizing Wings and Halos

1. **Wing Variations**
   - **Double-Layered Wings**: Use two cupcake liners of different sizes or colors to create layered wings for extra dimension.
   - **Feathered Wings**: Glue small white feathers to the back of the angel for a soft, ethereal look.
   - **Lace Wings**: Cut lace fabric into wing shapes and attach them to the back for a vintage, delicate style.
   - **Sparkly Wings**: Apply glue to the wings and sprinkle glitter over them for a shimmering effect.
2. **Halo Variations**
   - **Beaded Halo**: String small gold or silver beads onto the pipe cleaner before forming the halo.
   - **Ribbon Halo**: Wrap the pipe cleaner with gold or silver ribbon for a polished, elegant look.
   - **Twisted Halo**: Combine two pipe cleaners (e.g., gold and silver) by twisting them together for a multi-colored halo.

Creative Uses for Cupcake Liner Angels

1. **Tree Ornaments**
   - Attach a loop of string or ribbon to hang the angels on your Christmas tree.
2. **Table Centerpieces**
   - Arrange several angels in a row as part of your holiday table decor.
3. **Gift Toppers**
   - Place a cupcake liner angel on top of wrapped presents for a personal, handcrafted touch.
4. **Holiday Cards**
   - Glue a flat version of the angel onto cardstock to create beautiful, handmade Christmas cards.
5. **Classroom or Group Projects**
   - This craft is ideal for group activities. Each child can personalize their angel with unique decorations and colors.

Tips for Crafting Success

1. **Choose High-Quality Cupcake Liners**
   - Opt for sturdy liners with festive patterns or metallic finishes for a more polished final product.
2. **Pre-Cut Materials for Younger Kids**
   - For children who need assistance, pre-cut and fold the liners to make the process easier.
3. **Encourage Creativity**
   - Let kids experiment with different colors, textures, and embellishments to make their angels unique.
4. **Use Age-Appropriate Glue**

- Younger children can use glue sticks, while older kids or adults can use craft glue or hot glue for faster assembly.

5. **Organize Decorations**
   - Place rhinestones, sequins, glitter, and other embellishments in small containers to keep the crafting area tidy.

Advanced Variations

1. **Glitter Globe Angels**
   - Place a finished angel inside a clear plastic ornament ball to create a "snow globe" effect. Add faux snow or glitter for extra charm.
2. **Personalized Angels**
   - Write names, initials, or special messages on the skirt liner to make the angels personal.
3. **Light-Up Angels**
   - Insert a small LED tea light inside the cone to create a glowing angel for display.
4. **Holiday Garland**
   - String multiple cupcake liner angels together to create a festive garland for mantels or doorways.

Cupcake liner angels are a delightful craft that combines simplicity with elegance, making them a favorite among children and adults alike. Whether you create a single angel as a thoughtful gift or make a collection for decorating your home, this project is sure to bring joy and creativity to your holiday season. Encourage kids to experiment with colors, embellishments, and designs to create angels that are as unique as they are!

Chapter 8: Coffee Filter Snowflakes

Coffee filter snowflakes are a simple yet magical craft that transforms an everyday item into stunning holiday decorations. Perfect for kids and adults alike, this activity combines creativity and precision to produce beautiful, intricate snowflakes. These lightweight decorations can be used on windows, hung as ornaments, or strung together into garlands, adding a festive winter wonderland vibe to your home.

Materials Needed

To create coffee filter snowflakes, you'll need:

- **Round coffee filters**
- **Scissors**
- **Markers, crayons, or colored pencils** (optional for pre-decorating)
- **Glue or glue stick**
- **Glitter or glitter glue**
- **Small sequins or rhinestones** (optional for embellishments)
- **Plastic tablecloth or newspaper** (to protect surfaces during decorating)

Folding and Cutting Coffee Filters into Intricate Snowflakes

1. **Prepare the Coffee Filter**
   - Take a round coffee filter and flatten it out completely. Smooth the surface to ensure even folds.
2. **Fold the Coffee Filter**
   - **First Fold**: Fold the coffee filter in half to create a semicircle.
   - **Second Fold**: Fold the semicircle in half again to create a quarter-circle.
   - **Third Fold**: Fold the quarter-circle in half one last time, forming a triangular wedge.
3. **Draw a Design (Optional)**
   - For younger kids or those new to snowflake cutting, lightly draw patterns on the folded triangle with a pencil as a guide. These can include geometric shapes, zigzags, or curves.
4. **Cut Out the Snowflake**
   - Use scissors to cut along the edges of the folded triangle.
   - Experiment with different shapes: triangles, semicircles, or diamonds. Cut both the edges and the tip for more intricate designs.
   - Be careful not to cut too much from the folds, as this can weaken the structure of the snowflake.
5. **Unfold the Snowflake**
   - Gently open the coffee filter to reveal your unique snowflake design.
6. **Make Multiple Snowflakes**

- Repeat the process with additional coffee filters to create a variety of sizes and patterns.

Decorating with Markers or Glitter for Added Flair

1. **Color Before Cutting**
   - Use washable markers to color the coffee filter before folding and cutting. This allows the colors to spread slightly and create a tie-dye effect when unfolded.
   - Encourage kids to use winter-themed colors like blue, white, and silver or festive holiday shades like red, green, and gold.
2. **Add Glitter**
   - After cutting, apply glue to the edges or specific sections of the snowflake. Sprinkle glitter over the glued areas and shake off the excess.
   - For easier application, use glitter glue to outline or highlight parts of the snowflake.
3. **Use Sequins or Rhinestones**
   - Attach small sequins or rhinestones to the snowflake using craft glue to add a touch of sparkle and dimension.
4. **Layered Snowflakes**
   - Stack smaller snowflakes on top of larger ones and glue them together for a layered, 3D effect. Use contrasting colors to make the layers stand out.
5. **Create Patterns with Crayons or Colored Pencils**
   - Draw lines, dots, or patterns on the snowflakes with crayons or colored pencils to give them a personalized touch.

Creative Uses for Coffee Filter Snowflakes

1. **Window Decorations**
   - Tape the snowflakes to windows to create a frosty winter effect. Light shining through the filters highlights their delicate designs.
2. **Hanging Ornaments**
   - Attach a string or ribbon to each snowflake and hang them from ceilings, doorways, or Christmas trees.
3. **Snowflake Garland**
   - String several snowflakes together with yarn or fishing line to create a festive garland for mantels or walls.
4. **Gift Wrap Embellishments**
   - Use snowflakes as decorative accents on wrapped gifts. Tape or glue them onto the wrapping paper for an elegant touch.
5. **Holiday Cards**
   - Glue a snowflake onto folded cardstock to create handmade holiday cards. Write a heartfelt message inside and share with loved ones.

Tips for Crafting Success

1. **Choose Quality Scissors**
   - Use sharp, small scissors for precise cuts, especially for intricate designs. Rounded safety scissors are suitable for younger children.
2. **Protect Work Surfaces**
   - Lay down a plastic tablecloth or old newspaper to catch glitter and glue spills.
3. **Encourage Experimentation**

- Remind kids that no two snowflakes are the same, so every design is unique and beautiful.

4. **Organize Materials**
   - Keep scissors, markers, glue, and glitter in separate containers for easy access and cleanup.

5. **Practice with Scrap Paper**
   - If kids are new to snowflake cutting, practice folding and cutting with regular scrap paper before using coffee filters.

Advanced Variations

1. **Painted Snowflakes**
   - Use watercolor paints to lightly color the coffee filters before cutting. The thin paper absorbs the paint, creating a soft, blended effect.

2. **Glowing Snowflakes**
   - Glue the snowflakes onto sheets of translucent wax paper. Tape the wax paper to a window or hang it near a light source for a glowing effect.

3. **Snowflake Mobiles**
   - Create a mobile by suspending multiple snowflakes from an embroidery hoop or wooden dowel. Hang it as a centerpiece or in a child's room.

4. **Giant Snowflakes**
   - Use large basket-style coffee filters to make oversized snowflakes for bigger spaces like classrooms or hallways.

Coffee filter snowflakes are a simple yet versatile craft that encourages creativity and brings a touch of winter magic into your home. Whether kids prefer traditional white snowflakes or colorful, glittery designs, these handmade decorations are sure to add a festive charm to any holiday celebration.

Chapter 9: Mason Jar Lid Ornaments

Mason jar lids are a versatile and durable crafting material that can be transformed into beautiful, personalized Christmas ornaments. With their sturdy frames and smooth surfaces, they're ideal for showcasing photos, drawings, or even creating miniature holiday scenes. These ornaments are a delightful way to add a personal touch to your Christmas tree or to give as heartfelt gifts.

Materials Needed

For one mason jar lid ornament, you'll need:

- **Mason jar lid and ring**
- **Photos, holiday-themed images, or white cardstock**
- **Craft paint (acrylic or spray paint)**
- **Markers, colored pencils, or crayons**
- **Glue (hot glue or craft glue)**
- **Scissors**
- **String, twine, or ribbon** (for hanging the ornament)
- **Decorative embellishments**:
    - Glitter, sequins, or rhinestones
    - Miniature figurines or Christmas decorations
    - Cotton balls or faux snow
    - Scrapbook paper or fabric
    - Buttons, beads, or bows

Turning Mason Jar Lids into Personalized Ornaments

1. **Prepare the Mason Jar Lid**
   - Separate the flat lid from the ring.
   - Clean both pieces with warm soapy water and dry thoroughly.
   - If desired, paint the ring or the flat lid with a holiday color (e.g., red, green, gold, or silver) and allow it to dry completely.

2. **Choose a Base Design**
   - Decide whether the ornament will feature a photo, drawing, or mini Christmas scene.
   - If using a photo or drawing, trace the flat lid onto the paper or image and cut out a circle to fit perfectly inside the lid.

3. **Attach the Design to the Lid**
   - Glue the photo, drawing, or chosen design onto the center of the flat lid. Smooth out any air bubbles for a clean finish.
   - If you're creating a painted or drawn design directly on the lid, do this step before gluing it to the ring.

4. **Decorate the Edges**
   - Add embellishments around the edges of the lid to frame your design. Use glitter, sequins, or small holiday-themed stickers for extra flair.

5. **Assemble the Ornament**
   - Place the decorated flat lid inside the mason jar ring. Secure it with glue if you want it to be permanent, or leave it loose if you prefer flexibility.

6. **Add a Hanging Loop**
   - Glue a loop of string, twine, or ribbon to the back of the lid or the top of the ring. Ensure the loop is strong enough to support the weight of the ornament.

Ideas for Photos, Drawings, or Mini Christmas Scenes

1. **Photo Ornaments**
   - Use family photos, pet pictures, or snapshots of memorable holiday moments.
   - Add text or captions, like the year or a holiday greeting, using markers or stickers.
2. **Kids' Artwork**
   - Let kids draw festive designs, such as snowmen, Christmas trees, or reindeer, on white cardstock.
   - Preserve their artwork by gluing it inside the lid and adding a layer of clear-drying glue or sealant.
3. **Scrapbook Paper Designs**
   - Use scrapbook paper with holiday patterns (e.g., candy canes, snowflakes, or plaid) as a background.
   - Layer small cutouts, stickers, or stamps to create a dimensional design.
4. **Miniature Christmas Scenes**
   - Create tiny holiday dioramas inside the mason jar lid:
     - Use small figurines, like Santa, elves, or snowmen.
     - Add faux snow (cotton balls, glitter, or shredded paper) for a wintery effect.
     - Include small Christmas trees, wrapped presents, or even a tiny sled.
   - Glue the scene securely to the flat lid and frame it with the ring.
5. **Inspirational Quotes**
   - Write or print holiday-themed quotes or Bible verses, such as "Joy to the World" or "Peace on Earth."
   - Use elegant script fonts and embellish the edges with glitter or rhinestones.

6. Fabric and Button Designs

- Cover the flat lid with festive fabric and glue buttons, beads, or ribbons onto the surface to create a cozy, home-spun look.

Creative Variations

1. Double-Sided Ornaments

- Decorate both sides of the mason jar lid for a reversible ornament. Use a photo on one side and a festive pattern or drawing on the other.

2. Magnetic Lids

- Attach small magnets to the back of the lid so the ornament can double as a fridge magnet after the holidays.

3. Light-Up Ornaments

- Insert a small LED light into the lid design to create a glowing ornament. This works particularly well with miniature Christmas scenes.

4. 3D Snow Globe Ornaments

- Glue a piece of clear plastic or acetate across the top of the ring to enclose your miniature scene and create a snow globe effect. Add faux snow or glitter for extra magic.

Tips for Crafting Success

1. Organize Materials

- Arrange photos, papers, and embellishments in small bowls or trays for easy access during the crafting process.

2. Use High-Quality Glue

- Choose a strong adhesive like hot glue for securing heavy decorations, and craft glue for lighter materials.

3. Ensure Neat Edges

- ○ Cut photos and papers precisely to fit the lid using scissors or a craft knife.

4. **Encourage Creativity**
   - ○ Let kids explore different materials and layouts. Provide a variety of supplies so they can personalize their ornaments.

5. **Protect Your Workspace**
   - ○ Lay down a plastic tablecloth or newspaper to catch any spills or glue drips.

Advanced Techniques

1. **Etched Lids**
   - ○ Use metallic paint markers to draw intricate designs or patterns directly onto the metal lid.

2. **Layered Ornaments**
   - ○ Add layers of foam or cardboard to create a dimensional effect with your design.

3. **Vintage Aesthetic**
   - ○ Distress the mason jar ring with sandpaper or paint for a rustic, vintage look. Pair it with sepia-toned photos or antique-style designs.

4. **Holiday Countdown Ornaments**
   - ○ Create a set of numbered lids (1–25) for an advent calendar. String them together to form a garland, revealing one ornament each day leading up to Christmas.

Mason jar lid ornaments are an ideal combination of simplicity and creativity. Whether your design features cherished photos, colorful artwork, or intricate miniature scenes, these ornaments are sure to bring joy and a personal touch to your holiday decor. Each ornament tells a story, making it a memorable keepsake for years to come.

Chapter 10: Sock Snowmen

Sock snowmen are an adorable and eco-friendly craft that transforms old socks into cute, plush snowmen perfect for decorating or gifting during the holidays. With simple materials like rice and a bit of creativity, kids and adults can create unique snowmen full of charm and personality. This fun, no-sew project is easy to customize with scarves, buttons, and accessories.

Materials Needed

For one sock snowman, you'll need:

- **White sock** (cotton or polyester blend works best)
- **Rice** (for filling)
- **Rubber bands or thread**
- **Fabric scraps, ribbons, or yarn** (for scarves)
- **Small buttons**
- **Pins, beads, or black marker** (for eyes and nose)
- **Mini pom-poms or felt** (optional for hats and details)
- **Glue (hot glue or craft glue)**
- **Scissors**
- **Funnel or spoon** (to help fill the sock with rice)

Making Plush Snowmen with Old Socks and Rice

1. **Prepare the Sock**
   - Take a clean white sock and stretch it out gently. Ensure it has no holes to prevent rice from spilling.
2. **Fill the Sock with Rice**
   - Use a funnel or spoon to pour rice into the sock. Fill until you reach the desired size for the snowman's body.
   - Adjust the amount of rice for the bottom portion to create a stable base.
3. **Secure the Base**
   - Tie a rubber band or thread tightly around the sock just above the rice to seal the base. This will form the snowman's body.
4. **Create the Head**
   - Add more rice on top of the base, shaping a smaller ball for the snowman's head.
   - Secure another rubber band or thread around the sock at the neck to separate the head from the body.
5. **Trim the Sock**
   - Cut off any excess sock material above the head. This can be repurposed for the snowman's hat.

Adding Scarves and Buttons for Personality

1. **Scarves**
   - Cut a strip of fabric, ribbon, or yarn to use as a scarf.
   - Tie the scarf around the snowman's neck, ensuring it's snug but not too tight.
   - For extra flair, fray the ends of the fabric strip to create a tasseled look.
2. **Buttons**
   - Glue or sew small buttons onto the snowman's body in a vertical line.
   - Use colorful buttons for a playful look or black ones for a classic appearance.
3. **Eyes and Nose**
   - Attach small black beads, push pins, or buttons for the eyes.
   - For the nose, use an orange bead, pom-pom, or a small triangle of orange felt to mimic a carrot.
   - If using a marker, draw the eyes, nose, and mouth directly onto the sock.
4. **Hats**
   - Use the trimmed-off sock material to create a hat. Roll or fold it to fit the snowman's head and secure it with glue.
   - Add a pom-pom or tie the top of the hat with ribbon for a finished look.
5. **Optional Accessories**
   - Glue small twigs to the sides of the snowman's body for arms.
   - Add tiny felt mittens or gloves to the twig arms for extra personality.
   - Place mini holiday props like candy canes or a tiny gift box in one of the snowman's twig hands.

Creative Variations

1. **Colorful Snowmen**
   - Use patterned socks instead of plain white ones for a whimsical, colorful snowman.
   - Choose socks with stripes, polka dots, or holiday-themed prints for added personality.
2. **Snow Families**
   - Create a family of snowmen in different sizes by using socks of various lengths and filling them with different amounts of rice.
3. **Festive Themes**
   - Dress your snowmen for the season:
     - **Santa Snowman**: Add a red felt hat and a mini gift bag.
     - **Winter Wonderland Snowman**: Use glittery fabric for the scarf and hat and add small snowflake stickers.
4. **Scented Snowmen**
   - Mix a few drops of essential oil (like cinnamon, pine, or peppermint) with the rice before filling the sock. This will make your snowman smell festive and inviting.

Creative Uses for Sock Snowmen

1. Home Decorations
- Display your snowmen on mantels, shelves, or tabletops to add a cozy, handmade touch to your holiday decor.

2. Tree Ornaments
- Create mini sock snowmen with smaller socks and add a loop of string to hang them on the Christmas tree.

3. Gift Toppers
- Attach a sock snowman to the top of a wrapped gift for a personal, crafty touch.

4. Party Favors
- Give snowmen as favors at holiday parties or classroom events.

5. Keepsakes
- Write the child's name and year on the bottom of the snowman for a memorable keepsake.

Tips for Crafting Success

1. Secure Rubber Bands
- Make sure the rubber bands or thread are tied tightly to prevent the rice from shifting or leaking.

2. Choose the Right Sock
- Use socks with a tight weave to avoid rice spilling through the fabric.

3. Even Out the Shape
- Adjust the rice in each section to create smooth, round shapes for the head and body.

4. Supervise Younger Kids
- Help younger children with cutting and gluing, as well as handling small embellishments like buttons or beads.

5. Test Stability

- Ensure the snowman's base is heavy enough to stand upright. Add more rice if needed for balance.

Advanced Techniques

1. **Glow-in-the-Dark Snowmen**
   - Add a battery-powered LED light inside the sock before filling it with rice to make the snowman glow softly in the dark.
2. **Snowmen with Accessories**
   - Create tiny accessories like earmuffs using pipe cleaners and small pom-poms or glasses with thin wire.
3. **Weighted Snowmen**
   - Replace some of the rice with small pebbles or beans to give the snowman a sturdy, weighted feel, ideal for outdoor displays.

Sock snowmen are a delightful way to upcycle old socks and spark creativity during the holiday season. With their soft, plush bodies and endless customization options, these adorable snowmen are sure to bring joy and charm to your Christmas festivities. Encourage kids to experiment with colors, textures, and accessories to create snowmen as unique as they are!

Chapter 11: Christmas Card Collages

Repurposing old Christmas cards into collages or gift tags is a creative, eco-friendly way to upcycle holiday leftovers while keeping kids engaged in a meaningful craft. By cutting and arranging images, words, and patterns from cards, children can create unique, personalized artwork that tells a story. This project encourages imagination, resourcefulness, and storytelling while adding a personal touch to holiday decorations and gifts.

Materials Needed

For Christmas card collages and gift tags, you'll need:

- **Old or leftover Christmas cards**
- **Scissors**
- **Glue stick or craft glue**
- **Cardstock or thick paper** (as a base for collages or gift tags)
- **Markers, crayons, or colored pencils**
- **Ribbons, string, or twine** (for gift tags)
- **Stickers, sequins, or glitter** (optional for embellishments)
- **Hole punch** (for gift tags)
- **Ruler and pencil** (to measure and outline shapes)

Repurposing Old Christmas Cards into Collages or Gift Tags

1. **Gather Old Christmas Cards**
   - Collect Christmas cards from past holidays. Look for ones with colorful images, festive patterns, and holiday messages that can be cut out and reused.
2. **Cut Out Elements from the Cards**
   - Carefully cut out images like Santa Claus, snowmen, reindeer, trees, or ornaments.
   - Include decorative patterns, borders, and text elements like "Merry Christmas" or "Season's Greetings."
   - Cut smaller shapes, like stars or snowflakes, for accents.
3. **Choose a Base for Your Project**
   - **For Collages**: Use a piece of cardstock, cardboard, or thick paper as the foundation. Choose a color that complements your design.
   - **For Gift Tags**: Cut cardstock into smaller rectangles, circles, or other fun shapes. Punch a hole at the top for attaching string.
4. **Arrange the Cut-Outs**
   - Lay out the pieces on your base without gluing them down yet. Experiment with different layouts to create a visually appealing design.
   - Encourage kids to think about the story or theme they want to convey with their collage.
5. **Glue the Pieces in Place**
   - Once satisfied with the arrangement, glue each piece onto the base. Use a glue stick for paper elements and craft glue for heavier items.
6. **Add Decorative Details**
   - Enhance the collage or gift tag with additional decorations:
     - Use glitter or sequins to add sparkle.

- Outline shapes or write messages with markers or crayons.
- Add stickers or small bows for extra flair.

7. **Finish the Gift Tags**
   - Write the recipient's name and a holiday message on the back of each gift tag.
   - Attach string, ribbon, or twine through the hole at the top for easy attachment to gifts.

Encouraging Kids to Tell a Story with Their Art

1. **Create a Holiday Scene**
   - Ask kids to imagine a winter wonderland, Santa's workshop, or a festive family gathering. Use cut-outs from cards to build the scene on the collage base.
2. **Incorporate Characters**
   - Use images of Santa, reindeer, elves, or other holiday characters to create a story. For example:
     - Santa delivering presents under a starry sky.
     - Snowmen having a snowball fight.
     - Reindeer decorating a Christmas tree.
3. **Add Dialogue or Captions**
   - Write speech bubbles or captions for the characters to make the collage feel like a comic strip or storybook.
4. **Use a Timeline**
   - Create a sequence of events on a larger base, such as a long piece of cardstock or poster board. Each section can represent a different part of the story.
5. **Highlight Personal Experiences**
   - Incorporate personal elements, such as family photos or drawings, to make the collage reflect the child's own holiday memories.
6. **Encourage Collaboration**

- If crafting in a group, have kids work together to create a larger collage with interconnected stories or scenes.

Creative Ideas for Collages and Gift Tags

1. **Themed Collages**
   - Focus on a specific theme, such as "A Night Before Christmas," "Winter Wonderland," or "Holiday Traditions."
2. **3D Collages**
   - Add layers to the collage by gluing some elements on foam tape or small cardboard pieces to make them stand out.
3. **Miniature Art Pieces**
   - Create a series of small collages that can be framed or turned into a holiday gallery wall.
4. **Photo Collages**
   - Combine images from old Christmas cards with family photos to create a mix of personal and festive elements.
5. **Unique Gift Tags**
   - Use cut-outs of ornaments, snowflakes, or stockings to shape the gift tags, making them stand out on wrapped presents.
6. **Bookmark Collages**
   - Turn smaller designs into bookmarks by laminating the finished collage and punching a hole for a tassel or ribbon.

Tips for Crafting Success

1. **Organize Supplies**
   - Arrange scissors, glue, and decorations in small containers to keep the workspace tidy and accessible.
2. **Provide Guidance for Younger Kids**
   - Help younger children with cutting and gluing to ensure clean edges and secure attachments.
3. **Encourage Experimentation**
   - Remind kids that there's no right or wrong way to design their collage or gift tag. Every creation is unique!
4. **Use Recycled Materials**
   - Extend the upcycling theme by incorporating other recycled items like wrapping paper, ribbon scraps, or leftover stickers.
5. **Protect Your Workspace**
   - Lay down a plastic tablecloth or newspaper to catch glue drips and stray glitter.

Advanced Variations

1. **Interactive Collages**
   - Add movable parts, like a spinning snowflake or a pop-up Christmas tree, for an interactive touch.
2. **Magnetic Collages**
   - Glue the finished collage onto a piece of magnetic sheet to turn it into fridge art.
3. **Illuminated Collages**
   - Use a hole punch to create small holes in the collage and thread a mini string of LED lights through for a glowing effect.

4. **Holiday Cards from Collages**
   - Fold cardstock into a card shape and glue the collage onto the front to create handmade holiday greeting cards.

Christmas card collages are a fun and meaningful way to repurpose old cards while sparking creativity and storytelling. Whether crafting gift tags, decorative collages, or personalized keepsakes, kids will enjoy bringing their holiday imaginations to life. This eco-friendly craft not only reduces waste but also encourages kids to think creatively and express themselves through their art.

Chapter 12: DIY Gift Wrapping Decorations

Gift wrapping is an art that can transform a simple present into something truly special. Teaching kids to create their own bows, tags, and embellishments adds a personal touch to holiday gifts while fostering creativity and resourcefulness. With simple supplies like yarn, stamps, and stickers, children can craft unique decorations that make every package stand out under the Christmas tree.

Materials Needed

For DIY gift wrapping decorations, you'll need:

- **Cardstock or thick paper** (for tags)
- **Yarn, twine, or ribbon**
- **Stickers, stamps, and ink pads**
- **Glue, tape, or a glue stick**
- **Scissors**
- **Hole punch** (for gift tags)
- **Markers, crayons, or colored pencils**
- **Scrapbook paper or fabric scraps**
- **Small decorations** (e.g., mini bells, buttons, or pom-poms)
- **Glitter or glitter glue** (optional)

Teaching Kids to Make Bows, Tags, and Embellishments for Gifts

1. **DIY Gift Bows**
   Gift bows are a simple yet impactful decoration. Kids can easily make them with materials found at home.
   - **Classic Yarn Bows:**
     1. Cut a long piece of yarn or ribbon.
     2. Make two loops, cross one over the other, and pull tight to form a bow.
     3. Adjust the size and trim the ends for a neat finish.
     4. Add these bows to gift boxes or tie them around gift bags for a classic look.
   - **Layered Paper Bows:**
     1. Cut several strips of scrapbook paper, each about 1 inch wide and varying in length.
     2. Loop the ends of each strip toward the center and glue them down to form individual loops.
     3. Stack the loops on top of each other, largest to smallest, and glue them together to form a layered bow.
     4. Add a small circle of paper or a pom-pom to the center for a finished look.
   - **Pom-Pom Bows:**
     1. Wrap yarn around your fingers or a small piece of cardboard multiple times.
     2. Slide the bundle off and tie another piece of yarn tightly around the middle.
     3. Cut the loops and fluff them to create a pom-pom.
     4. Glue or tie the pom-pom to the gift for a playful and unique bow.

2. **Custom Gift Tags**

   Handmade gift tags add a personal touch to any present.
   - **Simple Cardstock Tags**:
     1. Cut cardstock into small rectangles, circles, or festive shapes like stars or trees.
     2. Punch a hole at the top for string or ribbon.
     3. Decorate with markers, crayons, or stamps.
     4. Write the recipient's name and a short message on the back.
   - **Stamped Tags**:
     1. Use holiday-themed stamps (e.g., snowflakes, Santa, reindeer) and ink pads to decorate the tag.
     2. Add color with markers or glitter to enhance the design.
   - **Fabric-Accented Tags**:
     1. Glue small scraps of fabric or lace onto the tag for texture and dimension.
     2. Use fabric with holiday patterns for a festive touch.
   - **Photo Gift Tags**:
     1. Print small photos of the recipient or family members.
     2. Glue the photo onto the tag and decorate the edges with stickers or washi tape.

3. **Creative Embellishments**

   Embellishments elevate gift wrapping with unique textures and designs.
   - **Yarn and Twine Decorations**:
     1. Wrap yarn or twine around the gift box in crisscross patterns for a rustic, cozy look.
     2. Add small decorations like bells or pinecones tied to the yarn.
   - **Sticker Accents**:

1. Use holiday-themed stickers to create a festive border or focal point on the wrapping paper.
2. Let kids layer stickers to build a scene, like a snowy forest or Santa's workshop.

- **Paper Cut-Outs**:
  1. Use cookie cutters as stencils to trace shapes like stars, trees, or snowflakes onto colored paper.
  2. Cut out the shapes and glue them onto the wrapped gift as embellishments.
- **Natural Elements**:
  1. Attach small sprigs of evergreen, holly, or cinnamon sticks to the gift for a nature-inspired look.
  2. Tie them with twine for a rustic finish.

Using Simple Supplies Like Yarn, Stamps, and Stickers

1. **Yarn**
   - Use yarn to create bows, pom-poms, or tassels for decorating gifts.
   - Wrap yarn in multiple colors around a package to create a striped effect.
2. **Stamps**
   - Choose holiday-themed stamps and ink pads in festive colors like red, green, and gold.
   - Use stamps to decorate gift tags or create patterns directly on plain wrapping paper.
3. **Stickers**
   - Let kids choose stickers to personalize each gift.
   - Layer stickers for added dimension or use them to create borders and accents.
4. **Scrapbook Paper and Fabric**
   - Use patterned scrapbook paper to make bows, tags, or cut-outs.

- Glue fabric scraps onto plain wrapping paper to create a quilted effect.

5. **Glitter and Sequins**
   - Apply glue in designs like stars or snowflakes and sprinkle glitter over the top for sparkle.
   - Use sequins to outline shapes or create shimmering accents.

Creative Wrapping Ideas

1. **DIY Wrapping Paper**
   - Use plain kraft paper or butcher paper as a blank canvas. Let kids decorate it with stamps, stickers, or hand-drawn designs.
2. **Themed Wrapping**
   - Choose a theme for each gift, such as "Winter Wonderland" or "Santa's Workshop," and create decorations to match.
3. **Interactive Wrapping**
   - Add puzzles, mazes, or riddles to the wrapping paper for an interactive unwrapping experience.
4. **Recycled Materials**
   - Use old newspapers, maps, or sheet music as wrapping paper for a vintage look.
   - Decorate with colorful yarn or twine for contrast.

Tips for Crafting Success

1. **Organize Supplies**
   - Set up a crafting station with scissors, glue, and decorations within easy reach.
2. **Teach Proper Techniques**
   - Show kids how to tie bows, cut shapes, or use stamps effectively.
3. **Encourage Creativity**
   - Let kids experiment with materials and designs. Praise their unique creations.
4. **Supervise with Glitter and Glue**
   - Use a plastic tablecloth or tray to contain glitter and glue messes.
5. **Prepare Ahead of Time**
   - Pre-cut basic shapes like tags or bow strips for younger kids to make assembly easier.

Advanced Variations

1. **Pop-Up Gift Tags**
   - Create 3D gift tags by layering elements with foam tape or folded paper.
2. **Light-Up Wrapping**
   - Incorporate battery-operated LED lights into the wrapping for a glowing effect.
3. **Handmade Envelopes**
   - Craft matching envelopes for gift cards or small notes using decorated paper.
4. **Holiday Characters**

◦ Transform wrapped gifts into characters like Santa, reindeer, or snowmen using paper cut-outs and accessories.

DIY gift wrapping decorations are a fantastic way to teach kids the value of handmade gifts while letting them express their creativity. From bows and tags to embellishments, these personal touches will make every present feel extra special. Plus, the joy of creating these decorations adds even more magic to the holiday season!

Conclusion and Crafting Tips

Crafting with kids during the holiday season creates moments of joy, strengthens family bonds, and allows children to express their creativity. The projects in this book have been designed to be simple, engaging, and rewarding, providing opportunities for children to develop new skills and build confidence while making festive decorations and gifts. However, crafting doesn't have to end with the holidays—these activities can inspire a love for creativity that lasts all year.

Encouraging Creativity Beyond the Holidays

1. **Seasonal Adaptations**
   - Many of the crafts in this book can be adapted for other holidays or seasons:
     - **Valentine's Day**: Make heart-shaped garlands, pink and red cupcake liner angels, or love-themed collages.
     - **Springtime**: Use pastel colors to create flower garlands, bunny ornaments, or Easter egg decorations.
     - **Halloween**: Turn sock snowmen into sock ghosts or jack-o'-lanterns.
2. **Everyday Crafts**
   - Encourage kids to explore crafting as a regular activity:
     - Repurpose everyday items like cereal boxes, jar lids, or bottle caps into creative projects.
     - Make personalized bookmarks, journals, or homemade greeting cards.
3. **Expand Skill Sets**
   - Introduce new crafting techniques like weaving, sewing, or clay modeling.
   - Provide different materials, such as air-dry clay, watercolor paints, or fabric scraps, to expand their creative horizons.

4. **Start a Crafting Tradition**
    ◦ Set aside regular crafting days as a family tradition, such as "DIY Saturdays" or "Creative Sundays."
    ◦ Encourage kids to create seasonal decorations for the home, giving them a sense of pride and ownership in their work.

Quick Cleanup Strategies for Busy Families

Crafting with kids is rewarding but can sometimes lead to messy aftermaths. With a few simple strategies, you can streamline cleanup and make crafting more enjoyable for everyone.

1. **Prepare the Workspace**
    ◦ Use a plastic tablecloth, old newspaper, or a large sheet of parchment paper to protect your table or work area.
    ◦ Provide aprons or old T-shirts for kids to wear as smocks to keep their clothes clean.
2. **Organize Materials**
    ◦ Arrange supplies in small containers or trays to keep everything accessible and reduce spills.
    ◦ Use zip-top bags or small bins to store leftover materials for future use.
3. **Have Cleaning Supplies Handy**
    ◦ Keep wet wipes, paper towels, and a small trash bag nearby to quickly clean glue spills, glitter, or paint smudges.
    ◦ For sticky hands, set up a small basin of warm, soapy water for kids to wash up after crafting.
4. **Encourage Team Cleanup**
    ◦ Make cleanup part of the crafting process by involving kids:
        ▪ Assign tasks, like collecting scraps, wiping the table, or sorting materials into containers.

- Turn it into a game by setting a timer and seeing how quickly everyone can tidy up.

5. **Simplify Glitter Use**
   - Pour glitter into shallow containers to minimize spills and have kids use it over a tray to catch excess.
   - Use glitter glue instead of loose glitter for easier cleanup.

How to Preserve Kids' Crafts as Keepsakes or Gifts

Crafting with kids often results in creations that are worth cherishing for years to come. By preserving their work, you can create lasting memories and thoughtful gifts for loved ones.

1. **Seal and Protect Paper Crafts**
   - Laminate paper-based crafts, such as snowflakes, collages, or gift tags, to protect them from wear and tear.
   - Use clear adhesive sheets or self-sealing laminating pouches for a quick and inexpensive option.

2. **Frame or Display Artwork**
   - Frame special pieces like collages, drawings, or Christmas card designs to turn them into wall art or seasonal decor.
   - Create a rotating display space at home, like a corkboard or string line with clips, to showcase kids' crafts.

3. **Store Crafts Properly**
   - Use plastic bins or large envelopes to store flat crafts. Label each container with the year or occasion.
   - For 3D crafts, like sock snowmen or mason jar ornaments, wrap them in tissue paper and store them in sturdy boxes.

4. **Transform Crafts into Gifts**
   - Turn kids' creations into meaningful presents:
     - Frame a child's drawing or painting as a gift for grandparents or relatives.
     - Use their handmade ornaments or tags to personalize holiday gifts.

5. **Photograph and Digitize Crafts**
    - Take high-quality photos of each craft to create a digital archive.
    - Compile photos into a yearly scrapbook or photobook, preserving the memory of their creativity without needing to keep every physical item.
6. **Use Crafts for Holiday Traditions**
    - Incorporate kids' handmade decorations into your holiday traditions, such as hanging their ornaments on the tree each year or displaying their snowmen on the mantel.

Final Thoughts

Crafting isn't just about creating beautiful projects—it's about fostering creativity, building memories, and encouraging self-expression. The holiday season offers a perfect backdrop for these activities, but the joy of crafting can extend into every season and occasion. By teaching kids the value of resourcefulness, imagination, and sharing their talents, you're helping them develop skills and memories that will last a lifetime.

Let this book be a starting point for your family's crafting adventures. With every bow tied, snowman built, or ornament made, remember that the process is just as important as the finished product. Embrace the mess, celebrate the creativity, and enjoy the shared moments of holiday magic!

<u>Message from the Author:</u>

I hope you enjoyed this book, I love astrology and knew there was not a book such as this out on the shelf. I love metaphysical items as well. Please check out my other books:

-Life of Government Benefits

-My life of Hell

-My life with Hydrocephalus

-Red Sky

-World Domination:Woman's rule

-World Domination:Woman's Rule 2: The War

-Life and Banishment of Apophis: book 1

-The Kidney Friendly Diet

-The Ultimate Hemp Cookbook

-Creating a Dispensary(legally)

-Cleanliness throughout life: the importance of showering from childhood to adulthood.

-Strong Roots: The Risks of Overcoddling children

-Hemp Horoscopes: Cosmic Insights and Earthly Healing

- Celestial Hemp Navigating the Zodiac: Through the Green Cosmos

-Astrological Hemp: Aligning The Stars with Earth's Ancient Herb

-The Astrological Guide to Hemp: Stars, Signs, and Sacred Leaves

-Green Growth: Innovative Marketing Strategies for your Hemp Products and Dispensary

-Cosmic Cannabis

-Astrological Munchies

-Henry The Hemp

-Zodiacal Roots: The Astrological Soul Of Hemp

- **Green Constellations: Intersection of Hemp and Zodiac**

-Hemp in The Houses: An astrological Adventure Through The Cannabis Galaxy

-Galactic Ganja Guide

Heavenly Hemp
Zodiac Leaves
Doctor Who Astrology
Cannastrology
Stellar Satvias and Cosmic Indicas
Celestial Cannabis: A Zodiac Journey
AstroHerbology: The Sky and The Soil: Volume 1
AstroHerbology:Celestial Cannabis:Volume 2
Cosmic Cannabis Cultivation
The Starry Guide to Herbal Harmony: Volume 1
The Starry Guide to Herbal Harmony: Cannabis Universe: Volume 2

Yugioh Astrology: Astrological Guide to Deck, Duels and more
Nightmare Mansion: Echoes of The Abyss
Nightmare Mansion 2: Legacy of Shadows
Nightmare Mansion 3: Shadows of the Forgotten
Nightmare Mansion 4: Echoes of the Damned
The Life and Banishment of Apophis: Book 2
Nightmare Mansion: Halls of Despair
Healing with Herb: Cannabis and Hydrocephalus
Planetary Pot: Aligning with Astrological Herbs: Volume 1
Fast Track to Freedom: 30 Days to Financial Independence Using AI, Assets, and Agile Hustles
Cosmic Hemp Pathways
How to Become Financially Free in 30 Days: 10,000 Paths to Prosperity
Zodiacal Herbage: Astrological Insights: Volume 1
Nightmare Mansion: Whispers in the Walls
The Daleks Invade Atlantis
Henry the hemp and Hydrocephalus

10X The Kidney Friendly Diet
Cannabis Universe: Adult coloring book

Hemp Astrology: The Healing Power of the Stars

Zodiacal Herbage: Astrological Insights: Cannabis Universe: Volume 2

<u>Planetary Pot: Aligning with Astrological Herbs: Cannabis Universes: Volume 2</u>

Doctor Who Meets the Replicators and SG-1: The Ultimate Battle for Survival

Nightmare Mansion: Curse of the Blood Moon

<u>The Celestial Stoner: A Guide to the Zodiac</u>

Cosmic Pleasures: Sex Toy Astrology for Every Sign

Hydrocephalus Astrology: Navigating the Stars and Healing Waters

Lapis and the Mischievous Chocolate Bar

Celestial Positions: Sexual Astrology for Every Sign

Apophis's Shadow Work Journal: **:** A Journey of Self-Discovery and Healing

Kinky Cosmos: Sexual Kink Astrology for Every Sign

Digital Cosmos: The Astrological Digimon Compendium

Stellar Seeds: The Cosmic Guide to Growing with Astrology

Apophis's Daily Gratitude Journal

Cat Astrology: Feline Mysteries of the Cosmos

The Cosmic Kama Sutra: An Astrological Guide to Sexual Positions

Unleash Your Potential: A Guided Journal Powered by AI Insights

Whispers of the Enchanted Grove

Cosmic Pleasures: An Astrological Guide to Sexual Kinks

369, 12 Manifestation Journal

Whisper of the nocturne journal(blank journal for writing or drawing)

The Boogey Book

Locked In Reflection: A Chastity Journey Through Locktober

Generating Wealth Quickly:

How to Generate $100,000 in 24 Hours

Star Magic: Harness the Power of the Universe

The Flatulence Chronicles: A Fart Journal for Self-Discovery

The Doctor and The Death Moth

Seize the Day: A Personal Seizure Tracking Journal

The Ultimate Boogeyman Safari: A Journey into the Boogie World and Beyond

Whispers of Samhain: 1,000 Spells of Love, Luck, and Lunar Magic: Samhain Spell Book

Apophis's guides:

Witch's Spellbook Crafting Guide for Halloween

<u>Frost & Flame: The Enchanted Yule Grimoire of 1000 Winter Spells</u>

<u>The Ultimate Boogey Goo Guide & Spooky Activities for Halloween Fun</u>

Harmony of the Scales: A Libra's Spellcraft for Balance and Beauty

The Enchanted Advent: 36 Days of Christmas Wonders

Nightmare Mansion: The Labyrinth of Screams

Harvest of Enchantment: 1,000 Spells of Gratitude, Love, and Fortune for Thanksgiving

The Boogey Chronicles: A Journal of Nightly Encounters and Shadowy Secrets

The 12 Days of Financial Freedom: A Step-by-Step Christmas Countdown to Transform Your Finances

Sigil of the Eternal Spiral Blank Journal

A Christmas Feast: Timeless Recipes for Every Meal

Holiday Stress-Free Solutions: A Survival Guide to Thriving During the Festive Season

Whispers of the Harvest: The Corn Mother's Journal

The Evergreen Spellbook

The Doctor Meets the Boogeyman

The White Witch of Rose Hall's SpellBook

The Gingerbread Golem's Shadow: A Study in Sweet Darkness

The Gingerbread Golem Codex: An Academic Exploration of Sweet Myths

The Gingerbread Golem Grimoire: Sweet Magicks and Spells for the Festive Witch

The Curse of the Gingerbread Golem

If you want solar for your home go here: https://www.harborsolar.live/apophisenterprises/

Get Some Tarot cards: https://www.makeplayingcards.com/sell/apophis-occult-shop

<u>Get   some   shirts: https://www.bonfire.com/store/apophis-shirt-emporium/</u>

<u>Instagrams:</u>
@apophis_enterprises,
@apophisbookemporium,
@apophisscardshop
Twitter: @apophisenterpr1
Tiktok:@apophisenterprise
Youtube: @sg1fan23477, @FiresideRetreatKingdom
Hive: @sg1fan23477
CheeLee: @SG1fan23477

Podcast: Apophis Chat Zone: https://open.spotify.com/show/5zXbrCLEV2xzCp8ybrfHsk?si=fb4d4fdbdce44dec

Newsletter: https://apophiss-newsletter-27c897.beehiiv.com/